purposes. We pray to ask for help, either for ourselves or for others. We pray in thanksgiving for blessings that have come our way or because what we asked for has happened.

We pray for forgiveness for the wrongs we have done – either to ourselves or to others.

We pray too because we can be lost and we need to express our feelings.

In my view God does not punish or condemn. God is a God who loves and a God who listens.

Yes, it is a great mystery In prayer we sometimes understand part of this mystery.

Tony McNeile

Personal prayer

Let us open our hearts to prayer.

The God of Love listens but does not speak, the God of Love moves but we do not see. The God of Love is - but has no form. In our prayer let us be aware of the God of Love listening and moving and being in our lives. Let us offer our silent prayers. We offer ourselves to be blessed by the mysterious God of Love.

Let us open our hearts to prayer.

To be given strength to deal with the challenges that face us; to be given strength to accept our weaknesses and manage in spite of them; to be given the strength to be humble and to be strong in our humility - listening to the sorrows of others rather than unearthing our own in competition. To be given strength to support our loved ones and all who are close to us.   To be given the strength to be positive in what we try to achieve.

Let us open our hearts to prayer.

The clock of time ticks away in our lives.   We watch the news and we see pictures of bad weather; we see pictures of fighting in foreign lands - We see the suffering caused by poverty and economic distress. We watch the kaleidoscope world from our chairs - and we wonder as the clock of time ticks away in our lives.

But there is a power beyond time.   A power we call the God of Love.   A power that gives the individual spirit strength to survive in this kaleidoscope world.   Gives power to the oppressed to stand up against oppression.   Gives power to the weary to carry on.   Gives power to see a future when life seems hopeless and lost.

The power we call the God of Love moves spirits to love humankind - to care for the wounded, to care for the sick, to teach the children, to support and champion the unloved and the unwanted refugees;

The power of the God of Love moves the spirits of those who love humankind.   They do not seek bonuses or rewards; they are not driven by the glamour and glitter of material wealth or station in life as a celebrity.   They do not sing of their own achievements. Their voices are rarely heard.

To the God of Love we give our prayer of thanks to those who carry that power in their spirits. We pray that we too may find that power within ourselves.   Whatever we do, however great or small our ability, let us show that the power of the God of Love is in our spirits. Let it shine in our eyes.   Let it echo in the words we speak.   Let it shine from the words we write.

So may that power grow in the world - touch every spirit where the clock of time ticks away in their lives.

Let us open our hearts to prayer.

We pray to the God of Love. Let us give thanks for the comforts in our lives - that we have warm clothes and warm houses and friends that we can rely on - and shops nearby for our food. Even when times seem difficult for us, we still have so much - let us be grateful for what we have.

And let us pray for those in other climes who are finding life difficult. Let us pray for them, send them strength through our prayers.

And let us think of those in our own country for whom cold weather is a living problem - families and individuals on low incomes.

Let our prayers reach out to those with authority, that they see with compassion, that they can understand the needs of people who find it difficult to make their own way in life. - that those who struggle with life should receive support and be understood.

Let us open our hearts to prayer.

There is a world without and a world within.   Let our prayer reach to that world within.

May it be a peaceful world filled with visions of places and peoples that are special to us. May it be filled with warmth and beautiful colours.   May it be filled with gentle pleasing soothing sounds.

May it be a place where angels walk and greet you with a smile. A place of peace.

The gate to this world is always open but not always easy to find.

If there are times when the outside world brings problems and anxieties, if there are times when the colours in the outside world are harsh and the sounds grating, let us go to the gate of the interior world - to be at peace and to consider what is going on in our outside world.   To look at it as a stranger would - without emotion. Let us feel the comfort of the friendly angels.   Let us feel safe from the worries of the outside but able to look at them.

The peace of the interior world can calm the storms outside, can show the paths out of problems.

Let us begin to build the interior world and let it help us to manage our lives in the outside world.

Let us open our hearts to prayer.

How great is the skill of the human mind and how creative when minds meet to plan and create machines and art that will benefit society, that expresses the hope and optimism of the generation, that reminds the present world of the successes and failures of the past.

Yet how sad when these skills are turned to creating weapons of war and destruction.

Our prayers are with those who are suffering in the theatres of war and conflict - their cities being shelled and bombed and the people there with nowhere to go. And our thoughts turn to all countries where there is violence and destruction.

We pray for peace and for reason to prevail in these sad places.

Let us open our hearts to prayer.

In our prayer let us bless our families and our friends. Let us bless the love we have for them. Let us send them our prayers of peace; send them our healing light. Let us send them our love and keep them in our thoughts.

Let us open our hearts to prayer.

When the way ahead is often dark, the path ahead unclear. We seek a path to understanding but our thoughts are stirred in turmoil and the light has flickered dim. We need to know the reasons but the truth looks only black.

When the world has stopped its turning and love is trapped within, we turn towards the darkness seeking a presence in our soul - a touch of reassurance and the words of 'Peace Be Still'

This is the God we pray to - to lead us through the pain;

This is the God of loving holding hearts within the darkness to comfort and soothe the sorrow and return the light once more,

This nameless sacred presence is greater than all other wandering thoughts.   Inspiring all to movement, wiping scales from tearful eyes.

So may we feel empowered to walk the lonely road, fall in with other pilgrims and build a world that's new.

To speak against injustice; to return the smiles of welcome; to fill the cup that's empty and nourish the empty plate; do all and what we can to help.

May we offer love and comfort; may we offer reassurance and hope where hope has gone.

When our heart says, what is our purpose?, may the voice from beyond the darkness speak quietly in our soul.

To say the world is waiting and light shines on the way.

Let us open our hearts to prayer.

In a tangled world where there is anger and life is bitter because of war or hunger or disease or persecution or sadness or disappointment, we pray for peace and comfort to come into the world.

When we look for angels coming down with swords, we look in vain, we pray for armies of righteousness to descend in fire, we look in vain - violence and punishment does not bring God into the world,

Our prayer is to the God of Love, who looks at the world with sorrow

Let us open our hearts to prayer.

Let us take these moments for a meditational prayer - to allow our thoughts to slow and our minds to become calm - let us connect with that spiritual part of ourselves - the inner part - the sacred part.

Let us feel a stillness within ourselves behind everything that is busy and moving in our minds.

This is the stillness we reach for. Within it is a profound love - a love that feels like God's love - that touches us with serenity and calmness - and generates a deep joy - a simple joy that gives a love for life and for the world in which we live.

Let us open our hearts to prayer.

Let our minds float - float away to a sacred place that we keep in our hearts. A place that is special to us. If it is a room, let us wander around in it with our minds eye, see all the precious things within it - the photographs and the gifts received. Feel the holiness of this place.

If it is an outside place, be aware of the feelings of space, and atmosphere, sounds and scents and colours and the beauty of the natural world, the wonder of how all of nature is connected - each and everyone plays a part.

Let these special places be sanctuaries to visit and build up - to be places for silent worship when you are in busy places; when you are in noisy places.

Let us feel safe and secure in our special places,

bringing into them only those we want to bring in.

And as our minds float let us give thanks that we have the power of imagination to make these special places and go to them on a minds journey.

That we have the power to go outside our bodies and in our minds eye see a friend, remember an occasion; to recall beautiful moments.

That we can connect into the great mystery of life and wonder of the world and the universe about us.

That in the world there is a universal love and in our minds a place to meet with God and receive love and blessings

Let us open our hearts to prayer.

Let us think of God's love like a light that brightly shines within us - that gives us an energy and a physical strength that is both shield and sword for us.

With the strength of this light within us let our thoughts reach outwards - riding on the beams of our hidden light.   Let them touch the people we care about, assure them that they are in our thoughts.

They are beams of light that have the power to heal - let their healing power touch the hurts and uncertainties of those who are close to us - light that same light in their hearts to help make them whole.

They are beams of light that can melt anger, deflate the torment of frustration - let that light shine where it must.

Let us feel that light in our hearts - and shine it outwards.

May we keep alive this sacred connection to God's light. May it bless us and all whom we love and cherish.

Let us open our hearts to prayer.

We connect our hearts and our minds to the great mystery of creation and life - to feel that within the whole of this creation and all of life, there is a common thread. It is found in the swirling gasses and dust of the most distant galaxies and it is found in the world beneath our feet and within our gaze - an energy - a spirit of perpetual change and transformation - an energy that fills us with wonder. An energy that connects all things together.

Let us open our hearts to prayer.

We can live in the bubble of our own lives - with our own dreams and our own thoughts; our own fears and our own loves.

Let us give thanks in our hearts for a greater sense of connection - to feel that within the mystery and within the perpetual changing world there is a force for good that moves it all along. That all things change for a purpose - even though we can be blind to what its purpose is.

Let us open our hearts to prayer.

The flame of spiritual love travels unseen within us. We take its light and all that it stands for to every place we visit. May we hold the light aloft and kindle the lives of all who seek the truth about wisdom faith and tolerance.

Let us open our hearts to prayer.

Let us reinforce the values that we set the tunes of our lives to.

Let us acknowledge in prayer that life for others can be as difficult as it can be for ourselves sometimes. We all have times of self doubt; we all have moments of anger and frustration; we all have moments of intolerance. We can be superior when we should be humble; we can be weak when we should be strong.

Let us resolve to try to be better - to try to overcome what is a weakness; to let go of what we think makes us special.

Let us reach for the goodness; let us encourage; let us be disciples of the way and apostles of truth.

Let us open our hearts to prayer.

If there are times when we doubt, if there are times when we fear; if there are times when we do not feel connected to anything but are locked in the world of our own struggles, let us look again at what is around us - at the sky and the gardens; at the stars and the pebbles in the stream - and reach for that mystery - that constant purpose in the changing world - and feel in it the presence of the spirit of unseen God and the messages of love - let us welcome all into our hearts and join in the chorus of life.

Let us open our hearts to prayer.

Let us draw into the circle of love an image of ourselves. Let the light shine on us - cure us of our ailments; strengthen us where we feel doubtful; give us confidence, give us strength. Let us see that when we engage with the world we have gifts to share; that the greatest of these is friendship and recognition of those about us who also live in our world.

Let us open our hearts to prayer.

Let us pray for the lonely and unhappy people who do not feel part of the life we share. The weak who do not know what to do and fall at every hurdle. Give them some confidence and self belief. Let us pray for those who seem to be drifting through life without direction, who are influenced by things that don't really matter, who bow to the pressure of their peers and do not know how to stand alone and be proud.

Let us open our hearts to prayer.

Let each heart be open to prayer to reach out into the space where the image of love waits to touch our spirits at a deep level, bringing comfort where there is sorrow, bringing a calm peaceful blessing to the worried and the agitated, gently guiding the troubled away from the dark valley of despair.

Divine love is a radiance that fills the heart with contentment, opens the shutters and brings sunshine into the shady rooms of our inner selves.

It beckons the eyes to look up and smile at the closeness of friendships and family ties; the comfort of home and shopping in the bag.

Life that is filled with joy can forgive all wrongs, can understand the frailties of sufferers that prevents their being able to forgive or to make a compromise. Frailty that closes a life in so that it only sees its own problems and never beyond.

      Our prayer is a prayer of peace for ourselves, to be blessed and to acknowledge the spirit of holiness within us.

      So may the love that shines on us, shine on all, bring joy to all, bring a peaceful life to all.

      Hearts filled with sunshine bring light to all. May we shine, may we be patient, may we be understanding, may we be helpful, feel the richness that the spirit brings. May we carry the blessing of God lightly on our shoulders and feel content.

Let us open our hearts to prayer.

We pray to the God of Love to be with us in our thoughts; to comfort us and to give us peace; to give us strength. When our everyday lives are filled with worry or we have so many things to do - so many things to care about - so many duties towards our families, let us feel that our energy is being fortified and sustained by the God of Love.

May we give thanks to the God of Love, even when all that we do seems to be of no avail; may we give thanks to the God of Love when there are times when we feel there is no purpose and no point in doing what we do - let us look beyond such thoughts to the beauty of the world around us; the tranquility of beautiful places, the memories of times and places that have filled us with love and with joy.

May we give thanks to the God of Love for our health -and if it is painful health let us find that inner strength and peacefulness to be able to manage it and remain patient with those who care for us.

May we give thanks to the God of Love for our families and may they always be special to us. Let us pray for them when they are sick or unwell.   May we rejoice for them when they have achievements they are proud of.

Let us open our hearts to prayer.

Let us pray for ourselves that whatever troubles we may have, we shall have the inner strength and will to overcome them; that whatever doubts we have about our abilities we will find an inner strength to overcome them; that whatever fears we have we will have the inner courage to face them.

Let us pray for ourselves that our love may be bright and untarnished; that we can love our families and our true friends unconditionally; that whatever difficulties they may get themselves into, our love will always be there - that we can advise and not condemn; and if advice is rejected, let us accept it with good grace and keep our love strong.

Let us pray for ourselves that we will remain interested in the world around us and in our family and friends, listening to what they say, hearing the hidden meaning sometimes offered in their words.

Let us pray for ourselves that we care for our health and well being and do not give up too easily. Let us care for our minds and our bodies as a holy temple to be cared for and not neglected. Let us remember it is said we are created in God's image.

Let us pray for ourselves, that our faith will remain strong within us; that the values and principles of our faith are real and not hollow; that by showing in the way we live and in the way we treat people we are proud members of our faith community.

Let us open our hearts to prayer.

As children return to school or start school for the first time or begin again at a new school, we pray that they will enjoy the new surroundings and settle in and make new friends quickly. May God bless our children and grandchildren, the nieces and nephews too.

Let us open our hearts to prayer.

May the God of Love find a place in our hearts to feel at peace. In our prayer we re-assert the values we try to live our lives by. We seek to view the lives of our friends with compassion and understanding and to be supportive of them.   We seek to walk in the world unafraid to speak up against unfairness and wrongdoing.   We seek to listen to the voices of others and not drown them in our own. We seek to be assertive and able to say No to the things which would weaken our strength and our firmness.   We seek to be charitable when those around us do not care. We seek to be balanced in our speech when there is prejudice and discrimination around us.

We seek to keep the God of Love in our hearts.   May that

love keep us strong, open our eyes to what is beautiful and just.

When we feel down or disheartened, when we feel weak or inadequate, when we feel illness and soreness leading us to despair and impatience, may we find time to pause - just for a few moments to remind ourselves of what lies within our hearts, feeds our spirits, gives us strength. When we are challenged let us feel the God of Love secure in our hearts.

Collective worship

Let us open our hearts to prayer.

We gather for worship. Pleased to meet our friends and catch up with news - let us begin our time together with some moments of silence.

To reflect about worship and meeting in this house of prayer - to be part of this congregation of different people yet all here for what this building offers - a feeling of peace - a closeness to God - a spiritual place where the inner words of our lives can be said and heard in love - a place to seek blessings - a place to pray - for ourselves and for others.

Let us open our hearts to prayer.

In this house of prayer our minds and our hearts can become calm - we open ourselves to the joy of singing, the sacredness of prayers and to words to reflect upon.   This is our house of prayer.

Let us pray with love for all people.   May we hold fast to our own values and beliefs.

Let us seek blessings on those who are close to us and on this Chapel which is a spiritual home for us all.

We open our hearts before the God of Love, let us seek that love as we go day by day; let it be a shadow of light behind our thoughts and within our actions.   May our everyday lives reflect that love into the world.

Let us open our hearts to prayer.

We pray together to influence the peaceful parts of people's minds - and let them turn from violence to dialogue, from hate to understanding, from anger to calmness. May there be tolerance in the world, acceptance of contrary views and different faiths.

We pray that leaders of faith will preach the message of peace which is found in their scriptures - we pray that they will lead their followers to the negotiating table and seek and end to sectarian violence.

Our prayer is for them to understand that the strongest leaders are the leaders who have preached about loving God, valuing their neighbours as themselves and who calmed the storms in life by saying - Peace - be still.

Let us open our hearts to prayer.

In the peace of this place let the mind be at ease - to let go of the wild thoughts that clutter our minds and hold us back. To calm the chattering monkeys that disturb our concentration. To let our minds step aside from all that is around us; from all that we have brought with us; from all that we have in mind to do - and let us just be. To float for these moments without anything - part of the great universe - part of the all; part of everything and part of nothing at all.

Let us open our hearts to prayer.

We are in the sanctuary of this Chapel where there are sacred memories of families and friends, where there have been rites of passage, where there have moments of spiritual insight, times when hope has been restored to broken hearts; times of great joy and celebration.

We give thanks to God for this Chapel whose door is open to all who enter, which demands no vows of allegiance, demands no conditions for entry - except you are willing to listen and understand and be peaceful.

This Chapel is a place of prayer and friendship where the soul can speak to God in prayer.

In our prayer we thank God that we have the freedom to be ourselves in this Chapel. We thank God for all that is good in our lives -

the comforts of home, family, friendships.   We pray that we can be strong in our faith - not arrogant or boastful or rude - but gentle and caring and helpful - that our faith gives us power in our lives to face all adversities and challenges. That the light that shines from us is not a hurtful light.

In our prayer we pray for others - for our families and friends who are facing difficult times in life - whether through illness or the tribulations of those close to them. May they have that inner strength that comes from the spirit and stand and face all that confronts them without flinching.

And we pray for the world where there is so much sorrow and conflict - may the angels of peace comfort the suffering.

May all share in the vision of a world that can be made into a garden of beauty that all can live in with safety - a garden of peace and health where all may feel the love of God close in their hearts.

Let us open our hearts to prayer.

Allow this place of peace to touch the spirit and recharge it with life, make the colours seen more vibrant, the sounds more melodic, the love richer. Here in his place of peace the old colours of life are smoothed down and repainted with a new freshness. The senses are rejuvenated, touch and taste, smell and sight are all returned. Here the spirit has moved closer to heaven, has been where the angels have been, has been within the sacred moment.

Let us open our hearts to prayer.

We come from our different homes. We might have had to rush; we might have been too early. We have things to think about; things that have to be done afterwards - or next week..

But now we are gathered for worship -

We have found the time to be in this chapel, amongst our friends and with the welcomed stranger.

Let us focus our minds on our worship

Let us be still; let us take in the quietness of this moment.

Here we are touching holiness; touching sacredness - connecting our minds and our hearts to the spirit of God.

Let us open our hearts to prayer.

Let us take some moments for reflection and meditation. Let us open our minds in this sacred place where we worship together and open a circle of love. Bring into this circle images of our loved ones and friends; bring into the circle images of those we know who are suffering - families who have lost children, victims of crime; sufferers of illness.

Let us think of them with compassion. Give our love and support to them. Let us pray to the God of Love to give them divine strength and divine love - that they may find the strength. That they may find joy; that they may find calmness. That no matter how the storms of life rage about them, they are in the boat where peace is still.

Let us open our hearts to prayer.

In the beginning the spirit of God moved across the waters and created heaven and earth. God was the breath of life that fills all living things. In the beginning too was the word - that was logos - knowledge - that came to show the spirit of humanity that the light of God was in all things.

The light of the word shines everywhere for those with eyes to see. The word of knowledge can be heard everywhere for those who have ears to hear.

The word has taught us to find the sacred in life and be open to its touch. The word has given us eyes that can recognise beauty and feel the wonder of it within our very beings. The word has given us the language of thought and discovery and a path to the future.

The breath of life and the word that is knowledge point to the mysterious origin of ourselves.

May we tune ourselves into that mystery. May we open our own spirits to let the light in; open our minds to let the word come in.

May that same light shine out of us into a world without word. May that same knowledge be a beacon of truth in the dark to beckon closed minds to open and to blossom with fruits.

Let us open our hearts to prayer.

Let there be peace within our hearts - allow all thoughts and worries to be put to one side - allow anger and restlessness to subside - it cannot stay in a place of worship.

Take time to think about our faith - the corner stone of our lives.   The faith that restores the broken heart, the faith that restores the weakened strength; the faith that tells us all is not lost, that hope remains in the world and hope lives on in our hearts.

Faith that leads us through the clouds of despair; that lifts us out of darkness into the coming dawn; faith that tells us that all is never lost.

Faith that walks with us as an angel, taking our hand, helping us along.

The stories of faith can be our own stories.   Looking back we can see the turning points and our footsteps carrying on.

And faith is simply something within us - connecting our own spirits to a spirit beyond which is holier and greater. Beyond and yet near; beyond and yet within all that we see and experience.

Let us celebrate the faith that makes our spirit bright within us. Let us celebrate the knowledge of that greater spirit beyond and near and within all things.

Let us open our hearts to prayer.

Let us begin with a short meditation. Just to sit quietly and focus on being in this Chapel - let all other thoughts subside - let them go to the back of the mind.

And in the silence of this Chapel, let our thoughts focus on our inner selves - on the quiet spirit within us. Focus on this centre and feel an inner peace that can rise up to fill all your thoughts.

Be aware of the peacefulness of this building - and its history. Think of the many prayers that have been said here. Feel the holiness that has come through prayer.

This is the place and the time to be closely connected to the faith of this place.

So let our quiet minds tune into this holiness - absorb it

into the quiet peacefulness of our inner selves.

Let us open our hearts to prayer.

May our faith be an inner strength - like a strong ship that can sail through storms as well as calm - that gives us confidence and a belief that the journey is worthwhile and we will arrive in good heart and with bright spirits.

In our times of joy let us pray for those who are not happy - those who are less fortunate; those suffering in the places beyond the relay of torches.

May we pray for peace in the world - everywhere.

And let us pray for a strong sense sense of community that all people of all races will be treated and respected as brothers and sisters - as individuals as valuable as ourselves.

Let us open our hearts to prayer.

Let us remember that
often on our life's journey there are
times of difficulty, times of not
knowing what to do next because of
worry. Times of illness and stress.

And times too of great
happiness and great joy. In our
prayer let us accept these two
extremes of human existence. May
we have the strength to manage
both - to share in the joy of good
fortune - and even when our own
times are not so good to
acknowledge the joy of others and
not begrudge them their happiness.

Let us open our hearts to prayer.

In this hour of worship let us tune our thoughts into what is sacred. May the peace of God be amongst us. If we have done wrong, may our regrets be real and may love be restored. May we seek to forgive those who have hurt us and seek to understand.

May we be kind and thoughtful towards everyone concerned with our lives. May we overcome our own self doubt and self consciousness and be assured in what we do.

Let us help and serve others with love in our hearts.

May we value and feel part of this community which is our chapel. May we be upholders of its values and champions of its identity as a home of free thinkers and individuals, that its common creed is respect for one another, service for the good of humankind in the light of a love that comes from the God indwelling in our hearts.

May our prayer and our worship unite us in the fellowship that is this Chapel.

Let us open our hearts to prayer.

Let us use the power of collective prayer to make changes. To pray for those who are suffering because of the acts of nature - storms, fires, earthquakes, pray for those stranded in isolated places. Pray for comfort for them, give them new hope, new chances. Pray to give the power of compassion to those who govern in places where tragedies have struck and to those involved in rescue and bringing in aid.

Let us open our hearts to prayer.

This is our holy day. To open our hearts before God. To confirm the connection we have and feel the joy of the presence.

Connected to our God we pray for ourselves, admitting the weaknesses in our living and our failures to do good. We resolve to do better and be honest with ourselves, giving thanks for the connection to our God.

We pray for those we love, those who are closely connected to our own lives. Our love bears the pain of their lives the sufferings and misfortunes, the frustrated plans and broken dreams, and our love shares in the joys, their achievements and their happiness. We rejoice in their successes. In our prayer we bless the connections to our loved ones and our friends.

We pray for the community of this Chapel, our regular friends and our occasional friends. We pray to be of service and value to one another, to be supportive and helpful, offering comfort and understanding, and we give thanks for the care and friendship which is the bedrock of this chapel.

Let us open our hearts to prayer.

On this holy day we thank God for the strength we receive to live our lives connected to that holiness and to one another.

May we give thanks to the God of Love for this Chapel and its community - for the friendship and support we find in it; for the work and time it gives to the local community.

May the God of Love bless his Chapel and all who serve it.

Let us open our hearts to prayer.

In our prayer let us thank those whose working lives are dedicated to the cause of caring for humanity - who represent the good way to live and work and care.

Let us pray for the ones who work as servants for the suffering - helping and caring and encouraging.

We pray that the God of Love will care for them all, make them stronger, make them braver, make them more loving in the charity they selflessly give. In our prayer we bless them too and give them our thanks.

Let us open our hearts to prayer.

Let us focus for a few moments on where we are. This Chapel has been a place of peace for centuries. People have come here seeking peace and tranquillity.

Let us be aware of this place – think about its healing properties – that it can calm troubled minds, that it is a place where you can speak to God in prayer. It is a place where you can be silent. It is a place where you can be joyful and thankful. It is a place to receive a blessing.

Let us open our hearts to prayer.

Let us be calm. Let us be still. Let us feel the holiness of this place of worship. This house of prayer has heard the voices of generations before us - heard their sorrows and heard their celebrations, heard their concerns and their pleas for assistance. They have prayed for peace. They have prayed for good to be done and for evil to be put down. When times have been hard, they have come here for comfort and reassurance. When times have been good they have come here with thanksgiving.

They have comforted one another. They have rejoiced in the triumphs of one another. This house of prayer has heard all their voices, known their emotions, lifted their hearts.

They have known the presence of God in this house of

prayer. They have known a greater love. They have been a community of trust and love.

So may we, who worship here, honour them and honour this house of prayer. May we be open to its story and the power that it contains to comfort us.

May we have the same trust, the same closeness, the same love for this house of prayer - that reflects from ages past the great love of God. May its presence have a place in our lives and our lives always a place within this house of prayer.

Seasonal Prayers

Christmas

Let us open our hearts to prayer.
In this time of preparation for Christmas, let us hold the story of the nativity in our hearts. Let us ponder its deeper meaning - the coming of light into the world; the reaffirmation of God's gift of love, the closeness of heaven when the night is longest and the winter coldest.

Let the story inspire us to be like the innkeeper and always try to offer something when someone asks for shelter from life. Let us be like the kings and not too proud to humbly offer a gift. Let us be like the shepherds who look into the sky for angels singing. Let us follow the way of the peaceful.

Let us open our hearts to prayer.

In our prayer let us think of those who were not able to be with us or share in our festivities. May our love for them continue to be strong. May our prayer be for them to be blessed and to have joy in their lives.

If we have regrets that we did not fully enter into the spirit of the days, let them float up to God and be extinguished and let us look to the future and feel burden free.

In our prayer let us think of those for whom Christmas with its festivities is a distressing time - bringing back sad memories or opening old wounds. May their lives find blessings away from the sad times - and may the angels guard them

And when the holiday is over and the world returns to work, let us keep in our minds that message of peace and goodwill towards mankind of which the angels sang. What the world quickly forgets may we continue to ponder in our hearts.

Let us open our hearts to prayer.

Let us give thanks in our prayer for the blessings we have received this Christmas time. For the companionship of family and friends - for the exchange of gifts; for making contact with old friends - for the mood of festivity. And if we have been disappointed, let us not have regrets or anger but find the courage and calm within ourselves to let go disappointment go. If plans have gone wrong let us have the courage to shrug them

New Year

Let us open our hearts to prayer.
The lights of Christmas are turning off, the darkness of midwinter is giving way to lighter days.   Families have gone home, life must return to normal.   We gather together again as a worshipping community; amongst friends, welcoming the stranger.

Let our minds and our thoughts find quietness in these moments, savouring what has been with love, looking at the future with calmness; being in the present moment with our faith.

Let us open our hearts to prayer.

Another year begins - with hope and optimism for change. In our prayer let us give our blessings and good wishes to all who are important to us in our lives. Let us wish them success and happiness. Let the love we have for them be stronger and more open. Let us love them without requiring that we be loved back in return.

Let us open our hearts to prayer.

At the turning of the year we can look back. There have been times of happiness but also of sorrow. Lives have changed in one way or another. There are memories to cherish and bitter memories to overcome.

As the year turns let us be aware of the slowly lengthening days, the promise of snowdrops and green shoots stirring out of the earth.

Let us look forward to the coming year. Accept that there will be changes as there will always be changes. There will be joys as well as sorrows. Let us look forward in a spirit of holiness with he presence of God beside us. With the strength of hat love in our hearts we can be a light in the world. We can give of our wisdom. We can understand. We can forgive. We can be patient.

So filled with the spirit may we face the coming year with strong hearts and walk though it with strong steps.

Meditations

    Let the mind float - just being - think of God
    - think of the love that is coming from God
    - like a light that has travelled for many years
    - like a sound that is a melody of prayer
    - like a touch that is healing
    - like a touch that is comforting

    Let the mind float - just being - think of good things
    - a kindness received
    - a smile received
    - a thoughtful act received.

    As the mind floats - just being - think of the joy in being helpful

- think of the joy in caring for another living being
- think of the joy in giving time for another.

Silence for a while

As the mind floats - just being - think of God
- think of the love that is coming from God
- like a light that has travelled for many years
- like a sound that is a melody of prayer
- like a touch that is healing
- like a touch that is comforting

silence for a while.

So let us remember our moments of being
- with the mind floating

- and the love of God very near.

Let us open our hearts in meditation. Let the breath be gentle. Feel the physical connection of our feet to the ground and our posture as we sit.

Let the mind drift away from the everyday and the real, drift away from pain and sorrow and unaccomplished tasks. Drift away thoughts led by words. Drift into a space led by feelings, a place where the spirit sighs with joy, where there is deep contentment. A place where the spirit feels beauty and is touched by love. A place of always peace, without a ripple.

Allow this space to touch the spirit with life.

Let us be quiet in our thoughts and let the spirit of holiness be in our hearts, touching us with peace, filling us with love for the world we live in.

When life is difficult, if we are ill or we are sad for another's illness, if we are hurt or hurt for another's unhappiness, if we are doubtful or concerned for another's doubting, let us turn to that spirit of holiness and allow its strength to flow in, giving us confidence, giving us courage, giving us power to talk, power to act.

Let us use prayer to reach towards that spirit, to speak our feelings in the silence of our hearts, to declare the thoughts that worry us, to say the words we dare not speak out loud, to share the secrets we cannot share with anyone else.

Through the spirit of holiness let us know the presence of God, God who is the formless, nameless loving presence that is part of us and part of everything around us, that lifts us up and shows us the light ahead when all around is dark God who is the vibrant energy of life and the strength of silence.

Let us be still and quiet for these few moments at the beginning of our worship. Let our anxious thoughts subside and feel that within us in a deep well of spiritual peace - whose water cools our worries and comforts our hurts. With our minds becoming still let us quietly embrace the holy and sacred history of this chapel - feel the love that is held in its walls, let it float around us with its many colours and its shaded light.

Let us focus our thoughts on the world in which we live - to be aware of the shapes and colours of nature; the delicate structures of the flowers that grow from such tiny seeds; the strength and longevity of great trees; the power of nature to nurture its seeds just about anywhere - whether in the cliff face or the desert. The majesty of birds in flight and the proudness of animals. All is connected to all; all is dependent on all. We witness the miracle of life and the spiritual forces that hold it all together across different landscapes and seascapes of the earth.

And humankind is both part of this spiritual and physical realm but also separate from it. Humankind has the power to destroy beyond its needs; is able to destroy the world as it fights its battles amongst its own.

And we know in our minds we have the choice to reject as well as receive; The human mind can be suspicious and hostile and it can be loving and protective. It can share a space or exclude from a space; with a look it can be friendly without cause; with a look it can be hostile without cause. The human mind has complex responses to what it sees and hears.

May we in our lives seek to be balanced. May we seek to be fair; may we seek to be honourable. May we seek to protect the world we live in and make it safer for following generations;

May we feel and recognise the divine touch of the spirit of life - not only in ourselves but in all that grow and live amongst us in the connected world.

In our busy lives that can be filled with pressure and lists of things to do, let us find a space - a space for peace and tranquility away from all the storms and all the threats.

Let it be a sanctuary that we keep in our minds, a paradise of our own that we can escape to, whether a garden filled with flowers or a sandy isolated beach with blue sea and gentle sun touching your skin, or a favourite room filled with favourite things.

Let this sanctuary be a place in our hearts, a place of closeness and loving sentiment that is essentially our own, where no harm can reach us no fear confront us.

A place that is close and easily visited. A place of peace to be found for a few moments every day, or when clouds begin to gather. A place for the spirit to know real peace, real love, real safety.

We are small in the great order of things. Hurricanes and storms rage around the world and humankind is weak against them. The power of nature is awesome and frightening.

We give thanks for the resilience of the human spirit that when catastrophes come, there are people willing and able to risk their lives to save others. That in times of greatest need, the greatest good comes out in people.

We remember that in many cases, their faith gives them the strength to go the extra mile in their saving efforts.

We pray that we too may have that inner strength to help others. It is often easy not to notice the needs of a suffering soul - when we know we could help. It is often easy to cross to the other side when the Samaritan calls for help.

And if there are times
when we need to ask for help, let us
not be too proud to ask.

Benedictions
May the blessings we receive from our chapel be part of our everyday lives. May we reflect the values of our faith to the wider world we live in, love for one another, compassion for suffering, a peaceful heart. May we think good thoughts, say good words and do good deeds and be worthy of the blessings we have in our lives.

Walk hand in hand with life, hand in hand with each other, hand in hand as a community.

Let us go in peace - enjoy the coming week - seek the positive in life, honour our friends and be proud of our ancestors.
May the God of Love bless our efforts and the work we do for

others - may there be joy in our selves and in those we love.

May the blessings we receive be passed on into the world

And may the God of Love bless this chapel.

May the God of Love guide us and bless us in all that we try to do for the good of the world we live in - and may the blessings that we receive - shine into the world day by day, week by week.

Let us go in peace - and in friendship with one another let us be people of faith; let us live by our values; let our light shine in the world.

May the light of faith, the light of peacefulness shine in our lives. May our words and our deeds be the actions of our spiritual strength. May the spirit of holiness be close to us in all that we do. May we be blessed and may we bless. May the love of God guide us and empower us always.

Let us go in peace.
Follow the paths of goodness, enjoy our lives, celebrate the joys of friendship and the love of family.

Jettison the bad thoughts each day early and carry on our lips and in the touch of our hands the positive touch of a person with a proud faith. So may we be blessed and we too be a blessing.

Let us go forward into the new year with optimism - to help one another, support our community, help those in need.

May we feel the love of God in our hearts; giving us strength and giving us courage to live joyfully in the world. May we be people of peace.

Let us go in peace. May our inner strength be strong, our love for life bright. Let us seek to find joy in all that we have to do.

And may the God of Love bless each one of us and may we reflect that blessing in our daily lives.

Let us go in peace. Take with us the blessings of God and distribute them in the world. May we enjoy peace and joy through the coming week - may we think good thoughts, say good words and do good deeds always.

Sayings

God is love; God dwells within us; is peace, is caring, gives us an inner strength; gives us courage.

May we be ambassadors of peace when times are troubled and ambassadors of hope when people are afraid.

Let our spirits be open to the mood of our worship and let us feel the quiet energy that comes from our being together.

We pray for our families and our friends. May they be content in their lives, able to face any challenges that life puts before them; may they have the courage to overcome the challenges that they sometimes lay before themselves.

Pray for all people who face change in their lives. May they face the change with courage and may they feel the support of loved ones as they go their new journeys.

Let us draw into our circle of love, those we see as strong and sufficient. Let us give them our joy that they are content; they are in our thoughts.